Creating the Digital Art Library, 2013 Edition

ISBN: 978-1-57440-251-3
Library of Congress Control Number: 2013948387
© 2013 Primary Research Group, Inc.

TABLE OF CONTENTS

INTRODUCTION

This monograph profiles the digitization efforts of eight North American university art, architecture, and design libraries. Conducted in the summer of 2013, the following interviews shed light on a wide range of programs and initiatives, exploring the challenges library heads have faced and the successes they have experienced in digitizing their collections. Interview subjects open up concerning their digitization endeavors, including what's being digitized, and covering their experiences with digital image collections such as ARTstor, the challenges of digitizing in-house against the prospect of outsourcing such work, potential licensing and copyright issues, marketing the library's digital collections via social media, equipment and staff matters, prioritizations, and more. The results represent a broad spectrum of digitization efforts in art libraries today, from the newly-initiated to the well-seasoned veteran.

CORNELL UNIVERSITY LIBRARY

We spoke with several members of Cornell University's Digital Scholarship & Preservation Services program, including Danielle Mericle (Director of the Digital Media Group), Jason Kovari (Metadata Librarian), and Steven Folsom (Metadata Librarian). The Digital Consulting and Production Services (DCAPS) program services the entire Cornell library system, facilitating collaborations within the library community in the creation and management of digital scholarly content and tools to support learning, teaching, and research. Mericle has been with the Cornell library system for ten years, the last seven serving in her current position. Kovari has been at Cornell for over two years, and Folsom for one year.

General Description

The library system at Cornell University is unlike most library systems, a widely distributed library model consisting of eighteen units that cumulatively rank as the sixteenth largest system in North America. As Cornell does not have department libraries, these libraries (or units) tend to be larger than most. With such a distributed model—from the John M. Olin Library (research social sciences and humanities) to the Albert R. Mann Library (agriculture, life sciences, and human ecology), the Harold D. Uris Library (undergraduate social sciences and humanities) to the Carl A. Kroch Library (rare & manuscript collections and Asia collections)—the university has gone to great lengths to consolidate its technical services. Reorganizations have been frequent. Despite this, DCAPS has existed for over ten years, a virtual group consisting of staff from multiple departments, including Library Technical Services, Cornell Library IT, and Digital Scholarship & Preservation Services. DCAPS services are available to the Cornell community as well as external clients. "We try to feed off a single point of service," says Kovari of the library system's digitization efforts—making DCAPS the centralized digitization destination for all eighteen units in the system.

Fine Arts Library

One such unit is the Fine Arts Library. Housed on the third floor of Rand Hall, and with additional holdings at the Cornell University Library Annex, the Fine Arts Library is renowned for its art, architecture, and urban and regional planning resources. The library was founded in 1870 and comprises nearly 237,000 volumes, growing by approximately 4,000 titles each year. Essential indexes, such as the Avery Index to Architectural Periodicals, Urban Studies Abstracts, and Art Full Text are available both online and in print. The library maintains five full-time employees, two part time employees, and some twenty student assistants.

Knight Visual Resources Collection

"The biggest digitization initiative that came out of the College of Art, Architecture, and Planning," recalls Kovari, "actually originated in the slide library, a separate unit from the Fine Arts Library called the Knight Visual Resource Facility. The facility created what is known as the Knight Visual Resources Collection (KVRC), a digital image collection that supports instruction at Cornell and is restricted to Cornell University faculty, staff, and students for educational purposes only. The collection boasts a broad range of materials, covering art history, architecture, landscape architecture, planning, maps, and other documentary materials—over 40,000 digital images in all. "That effort started in the mid-nineties," says Kovari, "headed by Margaret Webster, the director of the Knight Visual Resources Facility." Webster, who maintained an internal staff, retired in 2009 when the facility ultimately closed. The Library has since assumed maintenance and growth of the KVRC. Within the College of Art, Architecture, and Planning, however, the model is difference, and consists primarily of faculty-generated content that doesn't often get placed into the KVRC repository.

Luna Insight

While images in the KVRC are discoverable alongside other images, the collection itself is its own entity and is cataloged in a completely separate database known as PiCTor, a home-grown system built in collaboration with Princeton University in the late 1990s. Online delivery is through Luna Insight (and ARTstor). In all, the Luna Insight database organizes nearly two dozen of Cornell's digital image collections, highlighted by collections such as the KVRC, the Herbert F. Johnson Museum of Art, and the Rare Book and Manuscript Collections. Outside these collections, Luna Insight also hosts smaller, boutique collections, such as the "Beyond the Taj" collection, a set of photographs by the late professor Robert D. MacDougall depicting South Asian architecture and culture. The MacDougall collection consists of around 3,500 images, while another collection showcasing aerial photographs of the state of New York from 1938 to 1991 totals roughly 1,250 images in all.

ARTstor and Other Collections

In addition to Luna Insight, Cornell University maintains a subscription to ARTstor, a non-profit 501(c)3 organization with a mission to further education and scholarship through digital technologies. While ARTstor's database is vast—nearly 90 percent of the images in the KVRC facility were already present in ARTstor—there were collections and areas that remained underrepresented, and DCAPS is working to fill in those gaps. Colonial tapestries is one such area, as is pre-colonial through contemporary Latin American art. "There was also an effort out of the Classics department," explains Mericle, "[to digitize] about 5,000 images that weren't represented elsewhere." ARTstor isn't the only organization with which the Fine Arts Library maintains a relationship, either. Other subscriptions include Scholars Resource, Landslides Aerial Photographs, Archivision, Saskia, Bridgeman Education, and Archipedia. These are primarily on one-on-one contracts, but the library is also open to consortial agreements with peer institutions.

Digitization Requests

"[DCAPS] has an ongoing collaboration with the College of Arts and Sciences," says Mericle, detailing a collaboration that furthers the digitization of the teaching collections. "It's glorified copy work. The faculty brings [the work] to us." Still it continues to grow, and grow handsomely: in the last six months, the program has had 5,000 images requested by the art history faculty alone. The demand has grown so much that Metadata Services has recently hired a full-time image cataloger to shoulder the load.

Even still, the digitization work performed by DCAPS comes to the program via an array of sources. "[But] there are a lot of different streams that images might come to us," Mericle continues. While faculty requests from the College of Arts and Sciences are increasingly popular, other avenues readily present themselves as well. Mericle lists requests from Architecture and Planning faculty ("That can be supported by the dean") as a steady stream. "However," she cautions, "it is a cost recovery operation. Regardless of where these requests come from, funding has to come from somewhere." Although this model has been in place for over a decade now, sometimes it does stop projects. Resources for teaching imaging, however, generally prove easy to find. There also exists within the College of Arts and Sciences a competitive grant program. "Faculty can apply for funds, for anything from digitizing the films of a German filmmaker in the last twenty years to something more esoteric, like digitizing a collection of ancient coins." In all, this grant program has funded about twenty-five projects over the last three years.

Two library digitization projects in the last five years particularly stand out. The first was a partnership with Microsoft in 2008 to digitize a significant number of the library's public domain works and to put the volumes online using Live Book Search service, thus allowing global remote access to Cornell's collections. A few years later, Cornell University Library partnered with Google to make its collections available online via Google Book Search, extending the digital collection's overall reach and breadth. Both times, a sizable amount of materials were pulled from the Fine Arts Library.

In-House vs. Outsourcing

The Digital Consultation and Production Services program handles much of its digitization work in-house, manned by a staff of 4.5 FTE workers (not including metadata), although there are projects that are outsourced. "We do outsource all film (of the moving variety)," explains Mericle, "and we also outsource high volume projects, like the Google initiative." The digitization of periodicals, too, is commonly outsourced. While other areas of the library include video and audio in their collections, this is not the case for the Fine Arts Library. But this is something the library is exploring. As Mericle explains, audio/video is a recent area of growth in the library system, although DCAPS didn't want to tackle this until they were ready. Mericle cites preservation and delivery as the two biggest obstacles. "Until we had a preservation repository in place, it didn't make sense to embark heavily on digitization." However, she expects this to ramp up significantly in the next few years, and in-house audio/video digitization is currently in development. Here, Cornell is modeling its efforts on the cross-campus initiative of Indiana University. "The real question is funding for the broader libraries," Mericle says, "pulling together resources and support."

Access

"The library tries to make whatever is available publicly downloadable," sayKovari. While some collections—such as the KVRC and Archivision—are available only to the Cornell community, the library system upholds a classic library model where if the image is downloadable, it's free. Likewise, if an image is requested for publication, the library asks that it be contacted for proper citation. "But we'd like it to be more granular," says Kovari.

Cornell is one of ten developing partners for ARTstor's Shared Shelf program, a media management software that enables institutions to manage, store, use, and publish their institutional and faculty media collections within their institution or publicly on the Web, thus allowing for shared access across departments on campus and with peers institutions.

UNIVERSITY OF CINCINNATI COLLEGE OF DESIGN, ARCHITECTURE, ART, AND PLANNING

We spoke with Elizabeth Meyer, Visual Resources Librarian at the Robert A. Deshon and Karl J. Schlachter Library for Design, Architecture, Art, and Planning (DAAP) at the University of Cincinnati. Meyer has been with the library for nine years.

General Description

As one of the country's preeminent design schools, the University of Cincinnati College of Design, Architecture, Art, and Planning—or DAAP as it is commonly known—consistently ranks among the top programs in the country. In 2005, its graduate architecture program ranked second in the nation after Harvard. In 2008, DAAP's interior design program was rated first for the ninth consecutive year in *Design Intelligence*'s annual list of America's best architecture and design schools. Then in 2012, *Business Insider*, ranking the world's 25 best design schools, listed DAAP third overall, behind only Rhode Island School of Design (RISD) and Massachusetts Institute of Technology (MIT).

Behind any great academic institution thrives a great library, and the Robert A. Deshon and Karl J. Schlachter Library for Design, Architecture, Art, and Planning (DAAP Library) provides on-site access to nearly 100,000 monographs and bound journals, hundreds of cutting edge periodicals in print, and a growing special collection. Since opening its doors in 1996, the Aronoff Center for Design and Art has been home to the DAAP Library and all its holdings. Designed by Peter Eisenman, the center is one of four buildings that collectively make up the College of DAAP, and as its latest addition the building hosts not just the library but the college cafeteria, auditorium, art supply store, and photography lab as well. "We're in a much larger space now," says Meyer of the library's relatively new home, occupying 14,000 square feet in the 164,000 square foot center. Before the move in 1996, when the Visual Resource Collection successfully combined with the library, the library had made its home in a 1950s-style building on campus. While that building still exists, the library made the leap into the Aronoff Center, a building which linked together the four college buildings. According to the college's website, "the expanded facility has enabled all of [our] programs to be housed together under one roof for the first time in [our] over 75-year history."

The Library's Collections

"We collect in all those disciplines," says Meyer of the library's holdings in reference to the College of DAAP curriculum, from Design to Architecture to Art and Planning. One collection of note is the Artists' Books Collection, which gathers one-of-a-kind, limited edition items experimental in nature, showcasing avant-garde, modern, and conceptual artists such as Sol LeWitt, Edward Ruscha, and Dieter Roth. "Sometimes the artists use different techniques, or some pieces are handcrafted that make them significant," says Meyer. The collection focuses on the 1970s to the present, and as bookmaking is a major component of the DAAP curriculum, the library actively seeks out works of book art that "provide a rounded view of contemporary attitudes toward the book." Another noteworthy collection is the Emile Mâle Collection, consisting of over 1,000 books from the noted French art historian's personal library. As was Mâle's focus, these materials explore French

Gothic Art and Architecture and highlight the historian's significant contributions to 20th century art history.

The personal library of renowned local designer Noel Martin—Art Academy of Cincinnati instructor and freelance designer—is the focus of the Noel Martin Collection. The collection focuses on various elements of design, including logo design, graphic design, font and typography, typesetting, printing, and lithography.

The Slide Collection and Digitizing

In 1993, the DAAP Library adopted the college's 200,000-piece slide collection and renamed it the Visual Resource Collection (VRC). Shortly after, in conjunction with the library's move into the new Aronoff Center in 1996, the library and the VRC merged into one and over the course of the next decade the slide collection, an assemblage of copy stand photography, began to see its popularity wane. "There were no sources on the slides," says Meyer, "so digitizing was difficult." Eventually, in 2009 the DAAP Library's slide collection was moved and the next year the VRC evolved into a digital research lab complete with 14 large-format Macintosh computers, professional grade scanning equipment, and high-end digital imaging software. "So we stopped digitizing slides. There was just no call for it; no one used slides anymore."

In lieu of digitizing the library's slide collection, Meyer relates that the library has focused on digitizing things more closely connected to Cincinnati. "Architecture, planning, images that are unique [to Cincinnati]," she says. One such example is a collection of slides from the

Cincinnati Preservation Association. For forty years, the Association dispatched photographers throughout the Cincinnati area to take pictures of buildings believed in line to be torn down or to be otherwise historically significant. The Association agreed to allow DAAP Library to digitize these slides. "There are also collections from scholars and professors of their own photography," says Meyer, "and every once in a while we receive donations of architecture plans and landscape plans. We get these donations about a couple times a year."

Other collections are still ongoing projects. "We've been working with a professor's architecture and urban planning slides from all over the world." But the goal remains to prioritize the digitization Cincinnati-centric material. Says Meyer: "We do like to focus on Cincinnati because then we're creating unique materials. It's something that's not out there already." Overall, Meyer estimates the library has been digitizing for about a dozen years now. "Before I came here, they were digitizing just for the classroom. They weren't creating archival images, and they weren't cataloging. Now, we're cataloging for the future, archival quality images. We try not to digitize anything unless it's going to be added to our collection."

ARTstor and Other Digital Collections

DAAP Library has maintained a subscription to ARTstor since the digital library's launch in 2004 via a one-on-one contract paid for, since the database is considered interdisciplinary, out of the UC Libraries budget. "ARTstor has about 1.3 million images," explains Meyer, "so they probably provide about fifty or sixty percent of our collection." As such, when the library looks to undertake a digitizing project, it looks first to ARTstor to see if the images are already available there. "We ask ourselves if it's needed for teaching," says Meyer, "and then we'll check ARTstor to see if they have it." As with all ARTstor subscriptions, access to the database requires University of Cincinnati login credentials. In addition to ARTstor, DAAP Library has access to several other digital image collections, including AP Images, Bridgeman Art Library, and Oxford Art Online. Meyer adds that the library would "love to have Archivision," but ultimately the budget will not allow it. "But if a faculty member really clamored for [an image or set of images], we'd try and work something out with the department to see if we could split the cost."

Digitizing In-House vs. Outsourcing

Most of the DAAP Library's digitization work is done in-house. "We have students who help with the scanning," says Meyer, citing a Nikon slide scanner as an integral piece of equipment. For these duties, the library employs student workers: one grad student who works 16 hours per week, and another student who logs in 20 hours weekly. Meyer recalls the library did outsource slide work one time, but this was because they had received a grant for the work.

Digitizing in-house does present its hardships, however. For example, Meyer notes that books prove particularly challenging, "because we just have the flat bed scanner, not a book scanner. The binding is what gets in the way. So you just have to make do." While the library would like to purchase a book scanner, it's simply not in the budget. Also on the wish list is a more professional copy stand. "We looked into a large drum scanner," says

Meyer, "to handle things like architecture drawings, but we've found that they break down a lot." She notes that another library on campus—the Geology-Mathematics-Physics Library—has such a scanner that DAAP uses for jobs that demand it. But a higher end copy stand, with capabilities to scan large scale drawings, would be ideal.

In terms of what gets digitized, Meyer says there exists a backlog of images that need to be cataloged. "Even the most basic part of that would be selecting the images," she says. The most frustrating part, then, is trying to get faculty to go through the plans and determine what is the most significant. "I've been waiting for that to happen for two years now," although in the end such decisions are mostly the responsibility of Meyer herself. "Still, I'd like to have faculty input." Meyer enlists the help of a student volunteer to aid in the process, with the student acting as a liaison between faculty and the library in order to coordinate what images faculty want digitized. As the Visual Resources Librarian, Meyer serves the entire university's visual resources needs. "There's not really another person devoted to that," she explains. As such, she does entertain scanning requests from individuals at other libraries. "Because we're not a separate department, my focus is to serve both the community and the college of architecture."

Access and Exposure

Content digitized by the library is uploaded into LUNA, and all of the library's collected images are available either through this platform or through the DAAP Library Media Database Collection, a homegrown system. When it comes to exhibiting, however, Meyer sees room for improvement. "We've had a few [digital exhibits] in the past," she says, "using

Dreamweaver software. But it's so time-consuming that we haven't been doing many lately. Right now, we don't have a way to highlight a collection. We've been clamoring for this for years."

While the library does not maintain a Facebook page or blog, it remains active with LibGuides. "My page is called 'Media,' and it's the number one campus guide in the library," says Meyer. She notes that information regarding the proper citation of images is a popular search on the guide. In addition, the library also has been using Pinterest, using the platform to upload different images (mostly architecture) from the library's public collections.

WILLIAM R. JENKINS ARCHITECTURE & ART LIBRARY AT UNIVERSITY OF HOUSTON

We spoke with Catherine Essinger, Coordinator at the William R. Jenkins Architecture & Art Library at the University of Houston. Essinger has served in this capacity for eight years.

General Description

The William R. Jenkins Architecture & Art Library has been housed in the College of Architecture building on the University of Houston's main campus since the library's inception in 1985. Located on the first floor, the Jenkins Library maintains a collection of nearly 125,000 books, journals, DVDs, and other research materials. "The library is curriculum-driven," explains Essinger, "so the strengths of the library very much follow the strengths of our faculty." As such, Essinger cites 17th century Dutch as well as Renaissance and Medieval art history as particular assets to the library and its collections. "We also have a very large graphic design collection." Located right next door to the school of art, Essinger estimates that approximately 40 percent of the library is dedicated to architecture and 60 percent is dedicated to art. Prior to 1985, these art resources were located in the general library. Today, the Jenkins Library employs 3.5 full-time equivalent professional staffers, not including the student workers who work year-round.

Digitization Efforts

"So far we've concentrated on material from our rare books room," says Essinger of the library's digitization efforts. "We are gradually working our way through some special projects with that." In addition, the library organizes a competitive juried art exhibit each year that is open to students: jurors from the most recent competition—the competition is now in its sixth year—included "curators from the Menil Collection and the Museum of Fine Arts, Houston, as well as prominent members of the Houston arts community and UH School of Art faculty." The student art that's accepted by the jurors is then archived and made public. While Essinger admits the digital art exhibit is not as popular or effective as more traditional exhibits—"There are certain expectations for an art exhibit, drinking wine and being there," she offers, "so it's [comparing] apples and oranges"—she has witnessed it gaining momentum.

The library works with the Digital Services department of the central library in coordinating its digitizing efforts. As this is a relatively new department (established about five years ago), and serves the entire UH library system, Essinger admits the Architecture & Art Library had to endure some false starts along the way. "It had been in the works for a long time," says Essinger, "but we had to wait until [the department] was up and running." The first projects went up and were made public about two years ago. In architecture, there's a focus on local architecture. On the fine arts side, "it's a mix of interesting things we've been pulling out of the collection, without necessarily a unifying theme." In addition to digitizing existing materials, the library is also creating original content. "We've recently started an oral history project," says Essinger, "and we're doing another [original] photography project now."

All the digitization work for the library is done in-house, through the Digital Services department. "For the first couple of years we did it ourselves," says Essinger, "but that got handed over." As there is no digitizing department within Jenkins Library, Digital Services is much more equipped to handle all digitizing duties, including scanning. "[Digital Services] has so many more people to handle the scanning. But the library does handle quality control and metadata." Essinger reports that there have never been any issues or obstacles in keeping digitization efforts in-house.

Digital Image Collections

The Jenkins Library maintains subscriptions for digital image collections with three different organizations: ARTstor, Art Museum Image Gallery, and Bridgeman Education. Bridgeman proves to be the least utilized, with 1,617 hits in the last year, while ARTstor (20,690 hits) and Art Museum Image Gallery (22,032 hits) registered more than ten times as many hits. "There are some people on faculty who use only ARTstor," explains Essinger. "It's popular for class presentations." The library has been steady in its support of these three databases over the years. While ARTstor is a single subscription, access to Art Museum Image Gallery was obtained through a deal the library had with WilsonWeb, and Bridgeman was arranged through Oxford Art.

Access

All in-house digitization projects are made publicly available; none of them are password protected. Databases like ARTstor, on the other hand, are available only to University of

Houston faculty, staff, and students (or with proper University of Houston login credentials from outside the library). All available images are downloadable for free.

Digitization Priorities

Each summer, the library consults with the Digital Services department to choose the digitization projects the library wishes to undertake. “Generally three [projects] each year is the right amount,” says Essinger. She expects they could do a little more, but like most libraries, over the last few years the library has been short-staffed. Moving forward, however, there are hopes to expand to a fourth project each year. The projects are entirely Essinger’s to propose, and she is happy to report there are no issues in getting approval. “There is a board of people through which every proposal has to go, but I’ve never had a problem.” In terms of what affects her decisions, Essinger says she carefully considers the widest audience outside the college. Local architecture, for example, is a far-reaching subject, and widely popular in the Houston area. “We’re one of the first places people come to research Houston architecture.” Essinger also takes great care to identify collections that complement what has already been done. Along these lines, she cites a rare travel literature collection in Special Collections in the central library that has garnered particular attention internationally. As such, Jenkins Library is in the process of organizing a collection of Victorian travel photography in an attempt to piggyback on the popularity of this Special Collections collection.

In terms of smaller, more individualized digitization projects by request, Essinger surmises that students and faculty are still adjusting to the fact that the library is capable of this. “It doesn't occur to them that they can make requests." As such, the library has entertained few requests for specific materials to be digitized, although this avenue remains open.

Outreach and Social Media

The library maintains an active online presence, including a Facebook profile and a blog linked to the library's main website, and looks to use these tools to their full marketing potential. "We've decided to focus on marketing each collection in turn," says Essinger, "one at a time." For example, over the past few months, the library has been focusing on promoting a collection of architectural retail pamphlets. While there is a marketing committee, there is no official department for these matters. "We haven't quite done anything like this before," offers Essinger. "But we decided there was a need to market [the collections] more heavily." As such, every month Essinger has been ramping up the marketing on each collection. "At the end of the calendar year, we'll see the stats and see how successful the campaigning has been." She also sees a need to increase internal marketing as well, with presentations at faculty meetings. Other marketing tools at the library's disposal include a recent profile by the Society of Architectural Historians as well as a mention in the Association of Collegiate Schools of Architecture newsletter.

HOLLAND AND TERRELL LIBRARY, WASHINGTON STATE UNIVERSITY

We spoke with two key figures involved in the digitization activities at Washington State University's Holland and Terrell Library: Bob Matuozzi, Humanities Bibliographer and Subject Specialist, and Greg Matthews, Digital Projects and Metadata Librarian. Matuozzi, an academically trained archivist, has been with the library since 1995, chiefly serving in Humanities and Special Collections, while Matthews has worked in several areas at the library since 1998, including cataloging, reference, instruction, and technical support.

General Description

As the largest humanities and social science library on Washington State University's Pullman campus—the university's main campus—Holland and Terrell Library serves the College of Liberal Arts and the College of Business and Economics, as well as departments in the College of Agriculture, Human, and Natural Resource Sciences. Established in 1950 with the construction of the Holland Library, and then supplemented in 1994 by the Terrell Library (then named the "New" Library or "Holland Addition"), the library is a desirable location for both study and relaxation. "One of the library's strengths," explains Matthews, "is it's location in the heart of campus." All of its materials are housed in the building, with no outside storage. Among other highlights, the library maintains government documents supporting the humanities and social sciences as well as education initiatives and a host of Pacific Northwest related collections.

The McWhorter Papers

"About two years ago," says Matthews, "we took a look at the landscape of digitization projects as they currently existed at the libraries." He explains there was a concerted effort by the dean to lend a higher profile to digitization at Washington State. "Our digital assets at that time came almost exclusively from [Manuscripts, Archives, and Special Collections]." "With no distinct digitization unit in the library," adds Matuozzi, "digitization efforts here really began with the appearance of the World Wide Web." As the pair relates, one of the first collections to be digitized at Holland and Terrell was the McWhorter Papers. The collection documents amateur historian Lucullus V. McWhorter's research and study of Pacific Northwest Native American history and culture. The collected papers span nearly an entire century, with particular focus on the late nineteenth century and up until McWhorter's death in 1944. Manuscript materials in the archive prove to be preeminent records of Indian history, tales, folklores, legends, customs, and languages, including transcriptions of oral histories and primary source materials of the 1877 Nez Perce War. An index and further information on the collection can be found here: http://ntserver1.wsulibs.wsu.edu/masc/McWhortr/Mcwh1.htm.

Unique and Idiosyncratic Collections

"Like any public institution [like WSU]," explains Matuozzi, "the one thing that's really fundamentally distinctive is the archives and special collections." From here the library had culled assorted Pacific Northwest materials, as highlighted by the McWhorter collection. But Holland and Terrell also boasts an array of idiosyncratic collections both curious and interesting to supplement the McWhorter Papers, all of which are managed via OCLC's digital collection management software, CONTENTdm. When the university's digitization efforts were ramped up, content that was not digitized elsewhere and was exclusive to Washington State was of particular interest. Faculty publications and uncommon journal titles, for example, proved to be key projects. There were unique collections maintained in a unique environment, such as a digitized print bibliography covering Lyme disease research and a complete digitization of the university yearbook, from 1895 to the present.

"As a land grant university, we play to the strengths of [WSU]" says Matthews. As such, Holland and Terrell's digitization efforts rely heavily on the opportunities that arise from coursework and other projects that are unique to the school. One such project is the digitization of a bulletin produced since 1913 by WSU Extension, which has offices all over the region. With this, the library digitizes both historical content as well as current content—the bulletin is an ongoing tool utilized by WSU Extension, both in print and the digital realm.

LandEscapes

When the dean of the university sought to formalize the then-amorphous digital projects unit in the libraries, one aim of these digitization efforts was to establish the library as a publisher in its own right. The focus here was on the digitization of the university's literary and arts journal, LandEscapes. Since its inaugural issue in 2000, LandEscapes has published all manner of fiction, nonfiction, poetry, art, photography, graphic novels, screenplays, and original works by WSU undergraduates—all of which formerly in print.

But now, in an initiative which has come to fruition in the last few years, the journal exists in the digital realm as well, thriving on a platform that allows personnel in the English department to do all the vetting and production work online. Likewise, content has expanded to include audio and visual, with the journal publishing student animation and music. Says Matuozzi of the digitization of LandEscapes: "It's been a huge success and has taken on a life of its own. It's opened up the campus publication to be truly representative of the campus." The magazine operates under the guidance of writer and Faculty Advisor Peter Chilson, and while content and maintenance is handled outside the library, in hosting the magazine the library is now acting as a publisher, drawing praise from Matthews as "the first instance of [the dean's] promise coming to life." While still available in print, the journal can now also be accessed online at the following address: https://openjournals.wsu.edu/index.php/landescapes.

Multimedia

Much like the LandEscpaes journal itself, the library's overall breadth of digital collections reaches beyond just still images and scans: WSU also supports a great deal of multimedia collections, including materials in film and radio. Of particular note is the J. Elroy McCaw Memorial Film Collection. Donated to the library by the family of the late broadcasting executive and station owner J. Elroy McCaw, the collection is comprised of four to five hundred acetate films. "They represent films that have otherwise been lost to history," says Matthews of these sole copies which feature not just B-list actors but the likes of Spencer Tracy and Peter Lorre as well. "The McCaws also gave the funds to digitize the collection," says Matthews, "and it's now all completely digitized and on DVD. Out next step is to be able to stream them."

In-House vs. Outsourcing

Most of the digitization work at the library has been performed in-house, and much of that work has been supported by transitory student help. "This is why the dean wants to streamline it," Matthews says. "These are the sorts of things that have been lacking." Matthews cites a need to create best practices uniformly across the board, as such practices would relate to sustainability and access. "These become even more important when you consider WSU as part of a consortium," and WSU is member to a consortium of over 30 libraries. As such, Matthews says the library is outsourcing "but in an internal sort of way." For example, the library received a donation of World War II internment camp photographs from a Japanese American family. With the donor insisting on a certain level of autonomy, the library partnered with Densho: The Japanese American Legacy Project, a nonprofit organization based in Seattle, Washington with an expertise in creating digital assets specifically regarding Japanese American internment. But as Matthews points out, such collaborations aren't the norm, and the prospect for outsourcing digitization projects is considered on a case by case basis.

Access

"From the library standpoint," says Matthews, "where we're putting images in CONTENTdm and describing that with metadata, that's available to everybody." Matthews posits that the library's general impulse is to provide resources it feels it has control over.

"That's what Research Exchange is for," he says, citing WSU's institutional digital repository. The Research Exchange is built to save, share, and search the university's research materials. Consisting of differing levels of access, content in the Exchange is set by the producer (i.e. the professor or faculty member adding the content). "But libraries are always interested in not only providing access to content for users but also then providing relationships with that content." Adds Matuozzi: "Our overall mandate is to provide services to students and staff of WSU, and then the citizens of Washington in general. But the advantage with digital materials is you can then make it available to the whole world."

Licensing, Copyright, and Image Selection

"That's the first question we ask," Matthews says of licensing issues with digitization projects. "'Does it have copyright and do we have to pay for it?' If the answer is yes, then we simply look elsewhere. That's one of the best practices we're trying to implement here." As such, copyright is seldom prohibitive when digitization projects are considered. More often than not, a lack of communication and an array of digital formats are the hurdles faced. "The [WSU Extension bulletin project] is something we've wanted to do for years and years," explains Matthews. "But we weren't able to get a handle on the entire run of the title." He admits there weren't high levels of communication and coordination at the Extension level with this, explaining that the Extension was having problems themselves with sustainability. "Lots of the bulletins they produce are revised over time," he says, with the original content then being destroyed. More technical problems also presented themselves, as some of these bulletins were published in print while others existed in microformat, thus necessitating the use of a $125,000 Zeutschel copier to digitize the latter.

Social Media

"In a lot of ways, the social media program is kind of ad hoc here," says Matthews. "There are some librarians that are more committed to social outreach than others." He adds that Special Collections maintains a Facebook page, but overall there's not an organized approach to social media.

The Future

"We feel pretty energized by the things going on here," asserts Matthews. "But it is difficult, even just between two people, to keep a handle on everything that's happening." Adds Matuozzi: "We work in a context, and our context is a state school in the Pacific Northwest. This is a state that's seen drastic cuts to higher education since the 2008 downturn. We're limited by both money and personnel. So we're an institution in flux, both stagnant and dynamic." There's a sense of urgency on the library's own sustainability as an organization. But still the future looks bright for digitization at WSU, as administration looks to integrate more fully the library with the digital movement. Consider the prospect of a digital humanities center, as proposed by the dean, which would potentially be housed in the library: "Partners from other parts of the university would have physical resources where their students could come to the library and create digital assets, assets that are not necessarily from the library," says Matthews. "The library would act as a digital resource."

ARCHITECTURE/FINE ARTS LIBRARY AT UNIVERSITY OF MANITOBA

We spoke with Mary Lochhead, Head of the Architecture/Fine Arts and Music Libraries at the University of Manitoba. Lochhead has been with the University of Manitoba since 1986 and has held her current position at the library since 1990.

General Description

The Architecture/Fine Arts Library at the University of Manitoba has been referred to as the second best architecture library at an academic institution in all of Canada, a claim with which Mary Lochhead is not one to argue. "Architecture is our strength," she says, citing very comprehensive and broad-based architecture and design collections. The library also supports the graduate level research needs of the Departments of Interior Design, Landscape Architecture, and City Planning as well as the School of Art studio art and art history programs. With over 90,000 volumes, the library takes full advantage of its home city of Winnipeg, the Chicago of the North. "Winnipeg has fabulous turn-of-the-century buildings," says Lochhead, and the library is used extensively by students in the program studying Winnipeg architecture.

For more than half a century, the John A. Russell Building on the university's main Fort Garry campus has been home to the Architecture/Fine Arts Library. Built in 1960, the Russell Building was the first building on a Canadian university campus designed specifically for a faculty of architecture. What started out as an architecture library became closer to what it is today when the Fine Arts Collection was welcomed into the library in the early 1970s. By the mid 1980s, the library had taken over the Faculty of Architecture's extensive slide collection, a collection of more than 125,000 slides at its peak. Today, the library employs two librarians and four full-time support staff members year-round, in addition to four or five part-time staff members during the academic term.

Digitization Efforts

The library admittedly has made few strides in digitizing its holdings, although the strides it has made have been significant. The most significant of its projects is the Winnipeg Building Index. Showcasing thousands of images, this ongoing database catalogs Winnipeg's rich and varied architecture, with references to further information in sources that include "monographs, journal articles, plans, images, and links to electronic publications and websites." After receiving initial grant funding from the Winnipeg Foundation, the Building Index continues to be maintained by existing staff—and Lochhead has her sights set beyond Winnipeg. "I hope to expand by scanning our Manitoba architecture slides," she says, adding that the database is due to be incorporated into the library's new digital asset management system. The database can be freely accessed through the University of Manitoba's website, or at the following URL: http://wbi.lib.umanitoba.ca/WinnipegBuildings.

The library has also digitized a large donation from the late Carl Nelson Jr., former faculty member in the Department of Landscape Architecture. As was Nelson's interest, the collection—known as the Gardens and Landscapes Image Collection—highlights the gardens of Italy. "While the intent had been to add to this collection," explains Lochhead, "the library was forced to dismantle the slide collection before this could be done." The collection can be found here: http://umanitoba.ca/libraries/collections/gardens/index.html.

Dismantling the Slide Collection

In May 2012, the Architecture/Fine Arts Library was forced to eliminate its slide collection. Says Lochhead: "We were occupying prime real estate in the building, and the space was required for the Faculty of Architecture. Neither the Faculty of Architecture nor the School of Art was interested in continuing to use slides and to provide the equipment for the classrooms." While the collection was at one time popular—Lochhead estimates that ten years ago 25,000 requests were made annually—usage had dropped to virtually zero. As such, with no one willing to support the equipment and no appetite to keep the material, most of the collection was discarded.

But not all of it. "I kept the slides of Canadian art and architecture, for sentimental and preservation reasons," says Lochhead. "There are cabinets [of the slides] in my office." Since future digitization projects remained a possibility, Lochhead was quick to hold onto these slides. Still other portions of the collection were relocated throughout various parts of the university. "We had a very good collection of Inuit art slides," she says, donated by the late scholar George Swinton. When the slide collection was dismantled, these slides were relocated to the university's Archives & Special Collections, to which Swinton had already donated large amounts of manuscripts and personal papers. Likewise, the library had previously managed a large collection of aboriginal art slides, which were relocated to the university's Aboriginal House, now called Migizii Agamik or Bald Eagle Lodge.

Concerning the demise of the library's slide collection, Lochhead has this to say: "It was a challenge for us because we were a slide collection in a library, not a slide collection in a faculty department." She explains this fostered a different kind of relationship with users from many disciplines across campus. "We weren't there solely to support teaching needs; we were there for broad-based research needs as well."

The library had also offered University of Manitoba faculty and students a scan-on demand service which, like the slide collection itself, was once popular but in recent years had seen its popularity wane. In the 2008-09 academic year, 87 requests were made and 1,255 slides were scanned. Yet these figures dropped precipitously to 45 and 459, respectively, for the 2010-11 academic year, and then down to 25 requests for 50 slides in 2011-12, the last year of its existence. "It was difficult to offer the quality of image people grew to expect," muses Lochhead.

ARTstor

The library maintains a subscription to ARTstor as part of a consortium contract. "We have ARTstor because it's so broad," says Lochhead, adding that the library hasn't had any requests from faculty for access to other data bases. However, she suspects ARTstor isn't utilized nearly as much by the library's patrons as it could be ("at least not as much as we'd like"), estimating that just 20 percent of wanted materials are obliged through the vendor's database, while the remaining 80 percent come from separate sources—sources such as the faculty's own scanned images and assorted resources off the internet. "I'm not sure where they're finding their materials," she says of faculty. In this way, along with the scanned documents from the erstwhile scan-on-demand service, the professors have over the years built their own collections of teaching materials.

When the time came to dismantle the library's slide collection, Lochhead says the first step was to compared the collection's images to the ARTstor database. "Our intention was to weed out what was duplicated in ARTstor, compress the collection, and find another location for it." This process of looking at the images took over a year. What the library concluded was that roughly 60 percent of the images in the slide collection already existed in ARTstor. "And we realized there was no point in keeping the remainder of the slides because there was no call for them."

Access and Copyright

The library's image collections require no login and are fully accessible to the general public. What's more, all images are downloadable and available in a variety of sizes. While the library does track overall website hits, it does not monitor download statistics. As is standard procedure, the library does ask that anyone wishing to use one of the library's scanned images in a publication first contact the library to arrange proper citation for the University of Manitoba. In regard to copyright, Lochhead says "we would not fill a request to scan a slide that had been copy photography (out of a book) or that we had purchased, because we had not purchased the digitizing rights." While the library still retains a slide scanner, its use is mostly relegated to the scanning of slide donations which, these days, are very infrequent.

Social Media and Beyond

Reference Librarian Liv Valmestad keeps the library active in the social media sphere, maintaining a blog, a Facebook profile, and a Twitter account. Valmstead uses these platforms to promote the library's collections and to keep the public informed of all library-related news and updates, including the library's database of scanned public art on campus. "Liv created a publicly available site showcasing campus public art, using QR codes," says Lochhead. She notes that Valmestad has written extensively about this public art database, including an article published in the Arlis Journal, *Art Documentation.*

UNIVERSITY OF FLORIDA DIGITAL COLLECTIONS

We spoke with Mark Sullivan, Unit Head of Digital Development and Web Development in the University of Florida Libraries Information Technology Department. Sullivan has been with the UF Libraries system for thirteen years, the last ten in his current position.

General Description

The library system at the University of Florida is as extensive and exhaustive as any system in the country. Consisting of nine libraries that collectively hold over 4.5 million cataloged volumes, 8.1 million microforms, 1.25 million documents, and 356 electronic databases, the libraries form the largest information resource system in the state of Florida. Eight of these nine libraries make up the George A. Smathers Libraries system—the ninth is the university's law library, the Lawton Chiles Legal Information Center. From within the Smathers Libraries system operates the University of Florida Digital Collections (UFDC), an ever-growing collection of digital resources from the UF Libraries as well as partnering institutions.

"About ten or twelve years ago," says Sullivan, "people started doing more digitization. At that time, we were hosting materials in a shared collection with other state universities in Florida. Then about eight years ago, we developed our own system." In 2006, UFDC was officially established on campus and today the collection, which includes books, articles, newspapers, photos, videos, audio, and more, boasts roughly 8.5 million pages and 300,000 items. "A lot of different projects have fit into it," explains Sullivan. "A lot of different grants."

UFDC's Collections

As UFDC hosts more than 300 digital collections, it is safe to say the collection's scope is broad, from curated collections (such as the art and architecture collections) to the institutional repository, which is hosted there as well. One such collection is the Digital Library of the Caribbean (dLOC), a cooperative digital library for resources from and about the Caribbean, which can be found at www.dloc.com. UFDC has also collaborated with the Samuel P. Harn Museum. Located in the University of Florida's Cultural Plaza, the museum's numerous collections showcase photography and Asian, African, modern and contemporary art, and UFDC has undertaken several digitizing projects in partnership with the museum.

The collections at UFDC represent a myriad of provenances. Some collections come by way of grants. Others come by way of donations: "Most architecture collections," explains Sullivan, "have come out of special collections. Boxes we've received from architects. We've been digitizing these, mostly about the architects themselves. They're more biographical in nature." Other times, it's at the behest of faculty that materials get digitized, such as with the *Kenneth Treister Collection*. The collection, which features the architectural drawings, project files, correspondences, publications and writings, and photographs of 20th century Miami architect, sculptor, photographer, and artist Kenneth Treister, was the result of years of teaching materials. "[Treister] was a professor here, and he gave us money to scan all the slides he had been teaching from."

When it comes to the selection of what to digitize, Sullivan says a main consideration is based on what's used the most. "A lot of times—and with universities in general, as well—we digitize for preservation reasons. The more the materials are online, the less people are physically going through the boxes." Faculty requests are also quite frequent, as with the Treister collection. "[UFDC] doesn't choose anything itself," says Sullivan. "The requests come from library faculty. For example, an agricultural librarian will come with something to digitize from the agriculture library. Mostly for research and teaching."

Grants

Sullivan estimates that UFDC receives about three or four digitization grants each year, "although we don't get a lot of grants for architecture and art," he adds. Currently, UFDC is digitizing a collection titled *Unearthing St. Augustine's Colonial Heritage*, of which they are roughly halfway completed. The project is funded by the National Endowment for the Humanities and seeks to digitally preserve a collection of hidden and fragile resources related to colonial St. Augustine. Partnering with the St. Augustine Historical Society, the City of St. Augustine Archaeology Program, and the University of Florida's Government House, UFDC has plans to digitize 10,000 maps, drawings, photographs, and documents, all of which will be freely available online. The database can be found here: http://ufdc.ufl.edu/usach.

Another grant-funded project is the *Aerial Photography: Florida Collection*, which collects more than 150,000 aerial photos of Florida between 1937 and 1990, documenting the dramatic changes in the state's land use during that time. The collection was funded by three grants from the Library Services and Technology Act. The images in the collection provide some of the oldest land use/cover information available, and are used extensively in agriculture, conservation, urbanization, recreation, education, hydrology, geology, land use, ecology, geography, and history. "We get more grants for heritage materials," says Sullivan. For example, in support of the Baldwin Library of Historical Children's Literature (housed within the Department of Special and Area Studies Collections), UFDC received several periods of grants, thus providing access to rare and unique titles from the library's print collection. "A lot of materials from 1810, the 1840s," says Sullivan of the digitized materials, pulling from the library's collections of manuscripts, original artwork, and assorted ephemera such as board games, puzzles, and toys. This digitized collection now contains more than 6,000 images, including over 200 versions of *Robinson Crusoe*.

In-House vs. Outsourcing

The Digital Library Center, located in the main library, is the only such facility on campus, and with nine FTE staff members the center shoulders the main digitization workload for UFDC. "We started out doing everything in-house," Sullivan says of their digitization efforts. "But things got more complicated. Now we do some projects in-house, while some are done remotely and others still are outsourced." One main issue with keeping it all in-house is a matter of format. "We don't do microform here. And with brittle books, complexity is an issue. Where the resources are, that's another factor and a reason to do remote scanning."

However, for materials they feel need particular attention and cleanup to counter problems with aging, these actions are all performed in-house.

SobekCM

Both the UFDC and the Digital Library of the Caribbean (dLOC) are powered by SobekCM, the university's own homegrown software engine. Developed by Sullivan in 2005, the system went live April 2006 and has been released as open source software. As per the library's website, "SobekCM allows users to discover online resources via semantic and full-text searches, as well as a variety of different browse mechanisms. [The] repository includes online metadata editing and online submissions in support of institutional repositories." In addition to the University of Florida, SobekCM has been adopted by the University of London, the Shoah Foundation at the University of Southern California, as well a handful of museums in Miami, including the Wolfsonian-Florida International University.

Outreach and Social Media

UFDC maintains both a Facebook account and a Twitter feed to stay connected in social media. "We use it to promote upcoming events," says Sullivan, "such as a new collection, an exhibit, or else just general news of the library." UFDC also is in the process of updating its website. "One of the reasons we wanted to do this is to tie in more with our social media outlets." In addition to Facebook and Twitter, UFDC has a presence on both Flickr and Instagram. "We've loaded a lot of different collections into these things," explains Sullivan.

In terms of exhibits, Sullivan says the library has had an exhibits person for a little over a year now. "Her entire job is to do both physical and digital exhibits," he says. One such digital exhibit is the Herschel Shepard exhibit, an online exhibition documenting the work of the renowned architect, one of Florida's leading experts in historic preservation. The exhibition explores the conversation that occurred during three of Shepard's historic preservation projects: the ongoing Gamble Mansion restoration; adaptive use at Government House; and the reconstruction at Mission San Luis de Apalachee. In general, physical exhibition space exists on the second floor of Library East (about 300 square feet), as well as a few other areas scattered around the main libraries—and the digital exhibits usually expand on the physical, oftentimes due to limited physical space.

FOGELSON LIBRARY, SANTA FE UNIVERSITY OF ART AND DESIGN

We spoke with Margaret Van Dyk, Library Manager of Santa Fe University of Art and Design's Fogelson Library. Van Dyk has been with the library coming on two years, and has served in her current position for the past year.

General Description

Santa Fe University of Art and Design (SFUAD) is an institution in transition. While rooted in the history of New Mexico's oldest chartered school, St. Michael's College, SFUAD is still in its infancy. Founded in 1859 and granted a charter for higher education in 1874, St. Michael's College was the city's first formal school, a La Sallian institution. In 1966, the college assumed the name the College of Santa Fe, a moniker under which it would operate for nearly half a century. However, due to financial concerns, the college closed in 2009, thus paving the way for a reopening the next year as the Santa Fe University of Art and Design, a name which, according to the school's website, "reflects the mission and vision of the school while also recognizing and upholding the reputation of the college, students, alumni, faculty, and staff." The new name brought with it a new emphasis for the institution, showcasing a completely art-based curriculum revolving around the disciplines of contemporary music, creative writing, theater, studio art, graphic design, photography, film, and dance. Each department has its strengths, with a small faculty and a large adjunct, and several of the faculty stayed through the transition and are well-known artists in their own right. "Our film school has been getting a lot of recognition and support," says Van Dyk. "Robert Redford is providing scholarship funds."

In addition to Fogelson Library, SFUAD also maintains a few branch or departmental type libraries, all of which are housed in buildings separate from Fogelson. One such library is the Chase Art History Library, with resources for conducting research in the history of the arts, archaeology, anthropology, and history of the Americas. Students also have access to the Beaumont and Nancy Newhall Library, a closed stacks research collection that is one of the foremost information resources for conducting research in the history of and aesthetics of photography in the United States.

A Collection in Transition

"We are collecting in all areas," Van Dyk says of Fogelson Library, "all major fields of study, photography and art included." Before the school's transition, Fogelson acted as the main library for the College of Santa Fe, serving a broad liberal arts and humanities curriculum. The transition to support an exclusively art-based curriculum, as headed by Van Dyk, is ongoing and is by no means an overnight process. "My long range plan involves a five-year project," explains Van Dyk, "and this is just getting underway now. There were a lot of other things to get up and running first." Still, the library is fully operational and plays to a myriad of strengths. Fogelson's unique position straddling its current directive forward and the inheritance of the characteristics of its former institution makes for a one-of-a-kind collection. "For the most part, our print collections are strong," says Van Dyk. Since most of SFUAD's academic programs preexisted at the College of Santa Fe (film and creative writing, for example), good collecting practices had been well established. There is also a strong emphasis on materials in theology and psychology, which while tenets of the old College of Santa Fe curriculum, remain today in Fogelson. "We've gotten to the point in developing [at SFUAD] that we are now just beginning to be able to address this transition of the print collection."

Because these programs preexisted with the College of Santa Fe, Fogelson is ahead of the game in terms of appropriate resources for its art departments—all of which are undergraduate programs, although there is an eye for exploring Master's programs soon. "We have a good, strong set of databases," says Van Dyk. "Some on our own, some in consortiums. Like the New Mexico Consortium of Academic Libraries. We have addressed our electronic resources, and we can move forward with providing for the students' research needs." Van Dyk adds that she would like to see the library provide a more apparent access to SFUAD's students. Right now, Fogelson maintains a very large 180,000+ print collection, but only a small percentage of it—Van Dyk estimates thirty percent—is relevant to the college's updated needs.

The Slide Collection

While the College of Santa Fe had started on digitization, it had only one significant effort: to digitize the art library slides, a collection of images taken by both faculty and students. "In the transition," explains Van Dyk, "we've reduced in staff size quite a bit, and the art slide collection was moved to Fogelson." Van Dyk was tasked with taking over this extensive project, but staff and time are limiting factors. What's more, Van Dyk reports that she is yet to discover if these slides had been previously categorized in any way. "There are images professors have taken of artwork, as well as things from books. So care must be taken when it comes to copyright." Thanks to The Friends of Fogelson Library, the library maintains a subscription to ARTstor, its only image database, and Van Dyk is counting on the idea that by the time the library is ready to revisit its digitization of the slide collection for classroom use, the images will already be there in the ARTstor database.

Priorities and Digitization Selection

While the library is not currently digitizing amid the bustle of the transition—the school itself has only been in existence since 2010—it does havea list of priorities and goals. "Our number one priority," says Van Dyk, "is the transition of the physical print collection. We talk and we plan and we discuss." In the meantime, another big initiative involves switching library systems. The library has been in contact with OCLC with intentions of moving away from its current system, SirsiDynix. "[OCLC] is so advanced with their catalog and integration of materials," praises Van Dyk. "Perhaps moving to the cloud is the primary reason we did it, and we know, from talking with OCLC, that they're close to being able to allow us to upload images to the cloud." The library has set a live date goal of September 1, 2013 for its new system. "We're very concentrated on making sure the transition to OCLC is as smooth as possible."

For a small art school—SFUAD has around 500 undergraduate students right now, with 2,000 as an end goal, although understandably this is a slow process—Van Dyk has visions of providing digitized resources for the school's art departments very soon. "My strategic directions include trying to digitize local works, from students, faculty, and local artists." In order to do so, she is looking to create a digital lab, the kind of which does not already exist within the library. "That is a future goal, to have the capability to digitize here." Van Dyk adds that she is hesitant to send out digitization work, wishing to keep it as close to home as possible: "I want very much to keep this in-house, especially because of the nature of our slide collection. In my experience, unless [the digitization work] is overseen very closely, [outsourcing] results are not very good."

In terms of what is to be digitized, Van Dyk says she depends greatly on her colleagues, and the unit operates at a high level thanks to her staff's creative and critical thinking. "There are five of us altogether. I have some really great idea people here, one of which has been here for several years and the others came on board with the transition." Van Dyk relies a great deal on her staff's input, and then suggestions and proposals are taken to the next level: the associate dean. "It's been an interesting process to see," she offers. "There's so much structural work that needs to occur regarding campus communication and knowing what kind of library resources are needed. But we are creating a scaffolding on the campus, and I welcome any and all input across the campus."

Social Media and Outreach

When asked if the library maintains an active online presence in social media, Van Dyk's immediately reply is "absolutely," citing a Facebook page that's been in existence for more than three years and a blog. "We use it to make connections to the campus, to announce campus events. The goal is to tie all things SFUAD to library resources, and because our social networking librarian is who she is, she comes up with amazing, eclectic posts, unearthing treasures in the collection. The art students do appreciate her quirky humor." Van Dyk sees social media and the internet as essential tools in connecting with the student community, and is constantly reconsidering the library's approach with this: "One of my staff is making the argument that we need to revisit which social networks are relevant to the students. We need to focus on those that are more art-oriented."

Van Dyk also subscribes to LibGuides, and sees the system as an excellent model for sharing resources. "I have my eye on them and what they're producing," she says. "Their resource-sharing model is exemplary. I'm hoping something arises in the world of digitizing librarians that is similar to this, so that we can all stop pressuring ourselves to do it all."

The Future

"While I don't have a scheduled project," says Van Dyk, "and its still in the formative stages, there are two things we want to see happen once we get on the new OCLC system." First, the library wants to begin collecting footage of campus events and student performances. "We know they're being filmed, but we want to be a repository for these things. We want to house it and catalog it on our databases." Secondly, Van Dyk sees a need for information literacy instruction, particularly for incoming freshmen, and is interested in utilizing all available tools at her disposal, such as online tutorials and video productions. "And since we're an art school, we want to be creative with it. We get theater students to act it out and have film students shoot it."

VISUAL RESOURCES CENTER AT THE UNIVERSITY OF CHICAGO

We spoke with Amanda Rybin, Associate Director of the Visual Resources Center at the University of Chicago. Rybin has been with the center since 2008 and assumed her current position in June 2012.

General Description

Established in 1902 alongside the University of Chicago's Department of Art History, the Visual Resources Center (VRC) began as a glass lantern slide collection and experienced significant growth in the early 20th century, eventually evolving into a very large 35mm slide collection. "By the end," explains Rybin, "we had over 350,000 [35mm slides]." But the evolution did not stop there, and by 2010, with the slide collection officially relocating to the campus library, the VRC was ultimately rendered into an all-digital operation. Today, the collections comprising the VRC boast over 300,000 digital images.

The center's mission is simple: to support the Department of Art History and the Division of the Humanities with visual resources for study and teaching. "We describe it to patrons by saying we help instructors and their students find, create, and display images for teaching and research," says Rybin. The VRC has always been associated with the Department of Art History, located in the Cochrane-Woods Art Center on the university's main campus. The center's collections are based on the university's current coursework and thus play to those strengths, and while the VRC serves the entire humanities division as well as the art history department, Rybin estimates that ninety percent of the center's materials are in direct support of the latter. "But we're reaching out to other departments all the time," she says. As such, there are a few noted subject specialties that stand out: modern art, medieval art, Islamic art, and Roman art. "Those are the four big groups, with modern art being the biggest."

Collections

The VRC maintains seven main collections, all of which are made freely available to University of Chicago students, staff, and faculty via LUNA, and all but one of these seven have either been contributed from campus partners or otherwise purchased. This seventh collection showcases locally created content, made by the Visual Resources Center itself. "This is the collection used most often," says Rybin of the in-house creation, and with over 100,000 images, it stands as the second largest of the group. In addition to the in-house images, the collection also includes 16,000 images purchased from Archivision's Base Collection, a core architecture collection representing major Western sites.

The largest of the seven collections made available through LUNA, however, is the AMICA Library (Art Museum Images from Cartography Associates) which contains with nearly 114,000 unique American museum images. This collection is licensed through the main campus library and renewed yearly. Rounding out the center's LUNA collections are Saskia (30,000+ core art history images with works from over one hundred museums), a selection of images from Bridgeman Art Library (14,000+ images from all time periods and places), Korean History in Postcards (a collection of 7,372 postwar images purchased by the main campus library), The Renaissance Society Archive (nearly 2,500 images from the Society, with many exhibition photographs), and the Legacy Image Collection (low-resolution scans from the VRC's pre-LUNA digital image collection). These subscriptions or purchases are all obtained through one-on-one contracts, as opposed to consortium deals. "Occasionally we buy additional sets from elsewhere," says Rybin, "such as from museums, or scholars, when we're trying to plug in holes [in the collection]. Usually from requests from faculty or students when they can't find an image." In addition to these LUNA collections, the VRC assists patrons with access to ARTstor, a subscription database with over one million digital images (paid for by the library).

Digitizing In-House

All digitizing for the VRC has always been handled in-house. While the center does face challenges maintaining its in-house practice, it succeeds in accommodating nearly all its digitization requests. For example, the center recently entertained a request to scan an original piece of art that proved too big even for the center's copy stand, and while such requests don't crop up frequently, Rybin says they were able to refer the project to colleagues on campus. Other times, there have been projects that require a little bit of forethought and planning. "One student came to us with three-dimensional models, and while we weren't used to it, we were able to accommodate the request." Adds Rybin: "There hasn't ever been anything really too big to deal with."

In regards to the slide collection, Rybin comments that this extensive collection has been partially digitized and the digitization work remains, in part, an ongoing project. "We scanned original, on-site photography," she says. "But for things we had photographed from books and that we knew we could get a better digital image elsewhere, we'd rather go back and scan the book as opposed to the slide." Although just one faculty member continues to use slides (a relatively small selection of Renaissance and Baroque slides), there is still an ongoing effort to scan slides of Medieval art.

Equipment and Staff

The VRC is able to accommodate such requests thanks in part to a great upgrade to its imaging lab in summer 2012. Among the new equipment brought in was a Bookeye 3 R2 overhead book scanner. "The [3R 2] is so fast. We use it for books with really tight bindings, fragile books, and other large image requests." The Hasselblad Flextight X5 was another new addition to the lab, a high-end transparency scanner used for scanning slides and various different formats of film negatives. Also new were three Epson Expression 10000XL graphic art scanners. "These are our workhorses," explains Rybin. "Their primary uses are for our standard image orders. A lot of visual resource centers have these scanners." As mentioned earlier, the VRC also maintains a digital copy stand (with film or digital camera), used primarily for items that won't fit on the scanner or for three-dimensional objects.

Two full-time professional staff members (each with a Masters in Library Science) are employed by the VRC, along with one part-time staff member with an MFA in Photography who handles the photography equipment. There are also five or six undergraduate students who scan for the center every quarter (approximately ten hours per week) and two graduate students who translate and catalog (approximately five hours per week).

Image Selection and Digitization Requests

As the VRC's mission statement is to support the teachings and research of the university's faculty and students, the collection most immediately reflects the needs and requirements of the university's coursework, particularly the art history department. The center is also diligent in targeting areas that need developing. "Each year we look through the courses offered in art history," says Rybin, "to see if any topics or areas jump out at us, to see if anything is underrepresented." While not all faculty members will bring digitization requests to the VRC, and some faculty have collections they have brought over from other universities, the center has in place a series of guidelines outlining what can be reasonably requested. There also exists a certain hierarchy when it comes to requests at the center: "Usually professors are needing [the materials] in a timely fashion, so we take their requests first, along with grad students who are teaching." Those projects are top priority, followed by requests made by undergrads and non-teachers. "At times we've had to put our collection development orders on the back burners," says Rybin. "We'll always put teacher and student requests at the head of the line. A lot of times, with students, what they want to be able to do is use our equipment to scan images for class papers. And they are able to do so."

The Digital Scrolling Paintings Project and Other Grants

The VRC has worked on a couple of grants, most notably of late the Digital Scrolling Paintings Project in coordination with the Center for the Art of East Asia. "[The project] is a place for people who are teaching or studying East Asian handscrolls to view a high quality version of the image online," explains Rybin. Users can scroll through the entire image, inspecting it in great detail. The project came about when faculty teaching the subject experienced difficulties viewing images in full detail. "So we developed this website, separate from LUNA, and about half of which is fully available to the public." Those scrolls available to the public on the website have all been obtained from museums ("We negotiated the copyrights," Rybin says) in extremely high quality formats. The remainder of the collection consists of images scanned at the VRC, and these images are exclusive with University of Chicago login credentials. The project can be found online at scrolls.uchicago.edu.

Other grants have involved the VRC in more circuitous routes. "A lot of times we have faculty members who are working on grants and they'll come to us with just the digitization component of that: to discuss equipment, costs, and anything else pertinent in writing the grant." For example, one faculty member had received a grant to digitize 4,000 images of the work of Chicago photographer Robert Sengstacke, and the VRC provided equipment and student workers as part of the grant. "Once it's all ready," says Rybin, "we'll put it in LUNA in its own collection."

Social Media and Outreach

The VRC is active in social media and uses the web as an integral outreach tool. The center's website (arthistory.uchicago.edu/vrc) also hosts an associated blog, powered by Wordpress, which is updated two or three times each week, keeping patrons and users informed about new collections and offering insights on newsworthy and relevant items.

While the center, due to copyright concerns, is hesitant to jump into any of the digital heavy media outlets (such as Instagram), it does maintain a Facebook profile and Twitter account, both of which are integrated into the blog. "Twitter we use primarily as a way to follow other museums, libraries, tech bloggers," says Rybin. "We use it to get fodder for the blog, and to stay current."

The center is also active in on-campus outreach. Rybin notes that the center's heavy promotion period is in the fall, when there are new students (and faculty members) on campus. "We go to all the orientation sessions," she says. "Especially for Art History and Humanities." The VRC also makes a point to maintain a presence at such library sessions, when students are introduced to the library and its services. "It's important to look around campus and to see who you can partner with and how, through them, you can reach their existing audiences."

Advice

As a new director, especially, Rybin has much to offer in ways of advice: "One thing that's been really helpful is to do a survey of your holdings, equipment, and all of your student employees. Just to make sure you have a handle of what your resources are. We were able to get an upgrade to our lab last summer because we kept a handle on our statistics—how many visitors we had physically and online. These helped immensely in making our case for new equipment. Even if you don't think you need it, keep that data close at hand. And finally, make sure you promote your collections as much as you can. Even if you're busy and you think your collections are well used, you have to get them out to audiences."

www.ingramcontent.com/pod-product-compliance
Lightning Source LLC
LaVergne TN
LVHW061256100826
845148LV00008B/1150

* 9 7 8 1 5 7 4 4 0 2 5 1 3 *